Mermaid Tales from Around the World

Mermaid Tales from Around the World

RETOLD BY MARY POPE OSBORNE
ILLUSTRATED BY TROY HOWELL

SCHOLASTIC
HARDCOVER

SCHOLASTIC INC.
New York

Grateful acknowledgment is made for permission to use an adaptation of
"The Beautiful Girl and the Fish."
Copyright © Oxford University Press 1962.
From FOURTEEN HUNDRED COWRIES
by Abayomi Fuja (1962) by permission of
Oxford University Press.

Library of Congress Cataloging-in-Publication Data

Mermaid tales from around the world /
[compiled] by Mary Pope Osborne
illustrated by Troy Howell.
p.   cm.
Summary: A collection of twelve mermaid tales from around the world,
featuring such sources as France, Greece, and North Africa.
1. Mermaids. 2. Tales. [1. Mermaids. 2. Folklore.]
I. Osborne, Mary Pope.   II. Howell, Troy, ill.
PZ8.1.M5145   1992
398.21   92-30527
CIP
AC

ISBN 0-590-44377-1

12 11 10 9 8 7 6 5 4 3 2 1   2 3 4 5 6 7/9

Printed in the U.S.A.   36

First Scholastic printing, September 1993

Designed by Marijka Kostiw

Troy Howell's art was rendered
in pastels on museum board,
some with gold leaf.

For Susan Sultan
— M.P.O.

For Dilys
with appreciation
— T.H.

CONTENTS

INTRODUCTION

EARLY every culture in the world has developed legends about water maids. Whether they take the form of the fish-tailed sea nymphs of the ancient Greeks, the humanlike lake princesses of China, or the shimmering *Merrow* of the Irish — aquatic female spirits have been universally cherished and feared.

When I first began searching for tales about water maids, I expected to find the typical legendary heroine — beautiful, kind, and in need of rescue. What I found instead startled me: a fiercely strong female character. Universally. Regardless of which country she came from, the water maid was a force to be reckoned with. Self-assured, independent and self-contained, she determined her own fate and could wreak havoc as well as bliss.

In the French legend of Melusine and the Irish tale "The Enchanted Cap," the mermaid exacts a terrible price when her rights are violated. In the Ukrainian tale, "Nastasia of the Sea," and the Persian tale of the Sea Princess, each maiden allows herself to be won by mortal man only after he has gone nearly to the ends of the earth for her. In the Native American legend of "Menana of the Waterfall," in Hans Christian Andersen's "The Little Mermaid," and in the Nigerian folktale, "The Fish Husband," the mermaid ultimately succeeds in getting what she wants — even after it appears that she has lost everything. The mermaid can mercilessly punish those who displease her, such as in the Cornish tale, "The Mermaid's Revenge," and in the German tale, "The Mermaid in the Millpond." Likewise both the Japanese Sea Queen and the Chinese lake princess give generous rewards to those who help them. Even when she behaves thoughtlessly and cruelly, as in the classical myth of Galatea, the sea nymph still determines the fate of all those around her. There are no passive, sugar-coated heroines here. Sea maidens have full identities and are not afraid to show their bad sides as well as their good. They can be helpful, but just as equally harmful; healing, but just as easily destructive.

Only in the last couple of hundred years with the development of modern science has our belief in the mermaid's actual existence diminished. Still, she remains very much alive in our imaginations. Small wonder. Sea maidens are good for us. They connect us to the life-renewing qualities of water. They link us to the regenerative powers of the subconscious. They combat the bleak reality of our concrete jungles. They deepen our kinship with the wild. In these technological times, may these children of the sea continue to splash vigorously through our dreams and stories, reminding us we are all a part of nature.

At the conclusion of this collection, I've included notes which explain my sources for each story. In every case, I reworked the original, most often paring it down, dropping extraneous elements that interrupted the flow of the narrative or diluted the dramatic suspense. I hope that with each revision, I have been faithful to the spirit and voice of the original storytellers, so that in the words of W.B. Yeats, all the tales that I've gathered will:

> *"...Spread out their wings untiring,*
> *And never rest in their flight,*
> *Till they come where your sad, sad heart is,*
> *And sing to you in the night,*
> *Beyond where the waters are moving,*
> *Storm darkened or starry bright."*

"Teach me to hear Mermaids singing..."
—JOHN DONNE

Melusine was laughing with joy.

He gasped in horror.

Mystery of Melusine.

THE MYSTERY OF MELUSINE

French

ONCE upon a time, a French count and his son went on a boar hunt. Near nightfall, the two stopped to light a fire in the woods. As they were warming themselves, a wild boar charged out from behind the trees. The count's son, Raymond, immediately drew his sword and struck the beast. But the blade glanced off the boar and stabbed the count instead.

Raymond cried out in horror and rushed to the aid of his father. But it was too late; the count was dead.

Raymond wept with sorrow. Not only did he mourn the death of his father, but he also feared that his younger brothers would accuse him of murdering the count, for they were jealous of the inheritance that would be coming to Raymond when his father died.

In grief and despair, Raymond mounted his horse and fled the scene. Soon he came to a moonlit glade. A fountain bubbled in the middle of the glade. Its silvery waters flowed over the pebbly ground and around the feet of three women. Each woman had long, wavy hair and wore a shimmering white dress.

Raymond could not believe his eyes—was this a vision of angels?

One of the women, amused by the look of astonishment on Raymond's face, stepped lightly towards him.

"Who are you?" said Raymond. "And where do you come from?"

"I am Melusine," said she, and she put her finger to Raymond's lips. "Ask me not where I come from, and I will not have to lie to you. Just come sit by me and we will talk."

Raymond was enchanted by Melusine. He was flattered that she wanted to know him better. As he sat with her all night, he told her about the terrible accident that had just occurred.

"Return to your castle as if nothing had happened," said Melusine. "All the huntsmen have gotten separated from one another. When you arrive alone, no one will suspect that you were actually with your father when he died. Since his body will be found near the dead boar, everyone will think he fell on the animal's tusk."

Raymond was calmed by Melusine's advice. He had never talked with anyone who was more wise or charming. At dawn, as the fountain glimmered with rosy sunlight, he asked her to marry him.

"I will marry you," she said, "but only if you give me the land near this fountain and build a castle here for me. Then you must let me spend every Saturday in my castle alone. No one can intrude upon me that day."

Raymond agreed to Melusine's strange request. Then he returned home. He followed her advice, and all was well. No one ever suspected that he had killed the count.

Soon afterwards, Raymond came into his great fortune, and he married Melusine. After the splendid marriage ceremony, she said, "Now remember. You must never intrude on my privacy on Saturdays. If you do, we will be separated forever."

Melusine named her castle Lusignan, and the villagers called her the Lady of Lusignan. She was greatly loved and admired by all— even though, over the years, she gave birth to many monstrous-looking children.

No one could figure out why Raymond and Melusine's children were all so hideous. Raymond wondered if his wife's secret had anything to do with the children's strange appearances. Their first son had one red eye and one green eye. Their second son had one eye higher on his face than the other. Another son had long claws and was completely covered with hair. And another had a boar's tusk protruding from his jaw.

In spite of their deformities, all of their sons grew up to be outstanding men. Some went into the priesthood; some became warriors. Though Raymond was puzzled about his children's odd appearances, he was proud of their great accomplishments.

Indeed, Raymond felt very lucky. His love for his beautiful wife never diminished. He tried his best to be good to Melusine, and he *always* kept his promise not to disturb her on Saturdays.

One Saturday, however, one of Raymond's jealous brothers came for a visit. "Where is Melusine?" he asked.

"You know she keeps only to herself on Saturdays," said Raymond.

"Ah, you must listen to me," said his brother. "Some are spreading strange stories about her. You should follow her one Saturday and find out what she does."

"Oh no. I would never do that," Raymond said. "She will leave me if I spy on her."

"But everyone is trying to guess her secret," said Raymond's brother. "Some say a prince visits her castle on Saturdays. Some say she is a witch and meets with other witches on Saturdays."

Raymond ordered his brother to leave him in peace. But once he was alone, he could not banish suspicious thoughts from his mind. By Saturday, he was burning with desire to know Melusine's secret. Soon after she left the house, he decided to sneak over to her private quarters. He crept through the woods to the castle of Lusignan. When he arrived, he stood alone in the woods to watch for her.

Raymond saw no sign of Melusine or anyone else for that matter. No witches cackled; no foreign prince cavorted with her on the castle grounds. Indeed, there was a lonely feeling in the air: The fountain waters were still; the birds, silent.

Raymond almost went home. But his brother's words tortured him. He crept closer to the castle, then slipped through the front door. There was no sign of Melusine in the empty passageways; no sign of her in the empty kitchen quarters or the great hall.

Raymond tiptoed up a winding staircase. He did not find Melusine in her bedroom chambers or in the spinning room. Finally, the only room he had left unexplored was Melusine's dressing room.

The door to the room was locked. With his heart pounding, Raymond peeped through the keyhole. Then he gasped in horror.

Melusine was bathing in a large bathtub. The entire lower half of her body had changed into the huge blue tail of a fish! The scales of the fish tail shone in the sparkling sunlight.

Melusine was laughing with joy as she splashed about in the tub.

Trembling with shock, Raymond scrambled down the stairs. He ran out the front door and raced through the woods.

When he arrived home, Raymond had resolved *never* to tell anyone what he had just seen. Oddly enough, his horror of losing his beloved wife was greater than his horror of discovering her astonishing fish tail.

Raymond spent the rest of that evening trying to compose himself. When Melusine returned, just past the stroke of midnight, he greeted her as if nothing unusual had occurred.

Time passed, and Melusine did not seem to know that Raymond had peeked through the keyhole of her dressing room door. But one day terrible news reached the castle. One of their sons—the one with the boar's tusk—had attacked a nearby monastery and killed over a hundred monks. One of those murdered was his own brother.

When Raymond heard of the disaster, he sunk into a deep sorrow. What grieved him most was that one of his sons had died at the hands of another. At first, he wondered if this was punishment for his having accidentally killed his father. But then he began to wonder if perhaps this horrible event was punishment for Melusine's secret.

Once this suspicion took hold, Raymond could not shake it loose. Finally, when Melusine was trying to comfort him, he blurted out, "Away from me, you hateful serpent, destroyer of my kindred!"

Upon hearing these words, Melusine fainted.

Immediately, Raymond was filled with regret, and he desperately tried to revive his wife. When she woke, she began weeping. She embraced him and said, "Oh, my love, I must leave you now, for my privacy has been violated. You have stolen my deepest secret."

And with a wail of agony, Melusine rushed out of her house, leaving her footprint on the last stone that she touched.

That night in the nursery, a maid beheld a glimmering figure standing near the cradle of Raymond's youngest child. The figure looked like Melusine, though from the waist down she had a scaly blue fish tail.

The children's maid was so captivated by her vision that she was unable to cry out for help. At dawn she watched the mermaid kiss her child good-bye, then slip away. Melusine never again returned.

The castle of Lusignan stood empty in its lonely spot near the great fountain. For many centuries thereafter, villagers believed it to be haunted by the ghost of the vanished countess who was half human and half fish.

Menona of the Waterfall.
Sketched by T. J. Howell. May 18, /99

MENANA
OF THE WATERFALL
North American Indian

ANY ages ago, a little girl named Menana begged the Great Spirit to let her live among the stars.

"You can only travel through the heavens if you give up your human body," said the Great Spirit.

Menana agreed to give up her human body, so the Great Spirit allowed her to wander the sky.

But soon Menana grew bored with the stars. "I want to go home now," she told the Great Spirit.

"Oh, it is not that easy to become a human again," said the Great Spirit.

But Menana begged and pleaded until finally the Great Spirit said, "I will let you be a human again. But first you must return to earth to live among the spirits of the flood who will adopt you as their daughter. Then over time, you will develop a human body."

When Menana returned to earth, she lived beneath a great waterfall as a water spirit and, over time, her spirit body did begin to change. First it became the body of a fish. Then it began turning into the body of a girl.

Finally, when Menana was more human than fish, the Great Spirit said, "Now you can go live among people. As you live among them,

7

you will lose the rest of your fish body. However, you will not be completely human until you fall in love."

Soon thereafter, the ancient head warrior of the Ottawa nation stepped outside to look at the rising sun. To his great surprise he found a little creature standing before him. She was half girl and half fish. Her hands and arms were covered with glittering fish scales, and in place of legs, she had a fish tail.

"Who are you?" said the old man.

"I am Menana of the Waterfall," she said.

Without further questions, the warrior took Menana into his household and began treating her as if she were his own daughter. Though she was strange to look upon, he assumed she was a gift from the Great Spirit.

In fact, all the Ottawas thought Menana was a wonderful gift. They loved to hear her laughter, for it was as lovely as the song of a sparrow. They loved to hear her stories for they were as fantastic as moonlit dreams. They also admired the exquisite work she did with her hands, especially the robes she plaited with mulberry bark and the feathers of war-eagles.

As she lived and worked among the Ottawas, the scales fell from Menana's arms and hands, and her fish tail turned into a pair of human legs. Menana's spirit, however, remained as untamed as any creature of the sea. She passionately loved swimming in the rushing rivers and dancing in the torrents of the spring rains.

More than anything, Menana liked to slip away from the company of the Ottawas and go down to the great waterfall in the forest. There she bathed and sang and talked to the invisible spirits who had once been her family.

One day when Menana returned home from the waterfall, she found a group of Adirondack warriors smoking a peace pipe with her adopted father. Menana's eyes rested upon a handsome young chief named Piskaret. He was the bravest warrior of the tribe. His arm was the arm of a strong man; his arrow aim was the aim of a stalwart man; and his heart was the heart of a good man.

Menana stared straight at Piskaret without the slightest trace of fear in her eyes or the slightest blush to her cheeks. Then she walked straight up to him and said, "Tell me how I can win your love."

Piskaret was immediately taken with her. "I already love you better than any other maiden in the world," he whispered in her ear. "Come, marry me and live with my people."

Piskaret went on to paint the charms of his native land. As he described the tall oaks, thick glades, and winding rivers, Menana felt great love for him. She knew she was now a complete human being, alive to all the joys, fears, and sorrows of human life. "I will marry you," she said to Piskaret.

But the proud Adirondacks refused to sanction the marriage of the young couple.

"We have heard strange stories about her," their leader told Piskaret. "We know her people are not truly human. They are the spirits of the flood."

"Yes, they have drowned our warriors in the past," said another warrior.

"And they have rushed into our villages and brought harm to our crops," said another.

Piskaret begged to be allowed to marry Menana. "She herself has injured no one," he said. "Why must she be punished?"

But the Adirondacks would not allow their hearts to bend with pity. They drove Menana away from the arms of her beloved. When Piskaret tried to run after her, they tied him up and bore him away from the Ottawa village.

When the water spirits heard about what had happened, they vowed vengeance against the proud Adirondacks who had brought their daughter Menana such sorrow. Thereafter, a black cloud covered the land of the Adirondacks, and they began having many wars with other tribes.

As for Menana, after she was separated from Piskaret, her eyes lost their lovely light. Like a bird of night, she wandered the dark forest, singing a sad song. She no longer joined the dance of the maidens, nor did she plait her beautiful robes.

Menana spent more and more time sitting alone by the edge of the waterfall, telling her sad tale to the cascading waters and listening to the waters speak soothing words back to her.

One day, after spending an afternoon conversing with the waterfall, Menana rushed back to her village. Her friends were surprised to see such a happy look on her face. Smiling radiantly, she announced, "I am going to leave human life now and return to the world of the water spirits."

"Why? Why?" everyone wanted to know. They all felt panic at the thought of losing Menana.

"I cannot tell you," she said. "I can only say that I must leave now."

Though everyone tried to talk her out of her decision, Menana would not change her mind. Finally, the Ottawas had no choice but to follow her in a large procession through the forest to the waterfall.

No sooner had Menana reached the cascading waters, than out of the swirling torrent rose a host of fallen spirits. They moved like ghosts through the air and welcomed Menana into the water. She gave one last wave to her Ottawa friends, then disappeared forever.

Later that same afternoon, an Adirondack war party was canoeing down the river above the waterfall. The leader of the expedition was none other than Piskaret. When the war party was within bow-shot of the waterfall, the surface of the water was covered with the apparition of grisly heads. The water spirits had assumed the disguise of warriors. They grinned hatefully at the Adirondacks and waved their spears.

In the middle of the water spirits was Menana. When she saw Piskaret, her eyes shone with love. As the warrior ghosts began slaying the Adirondacks, Menana caught Piskaret in her arms. She shielded him from the sharp spears and pulled him out of the canoe and sank with him beneath the surface.

The water spirits turned the slain Adirondack warriors into eagles and forced them to dwell forever on a misty island which stood below the raging waterfall. An eagle's sense of hearing is so refined that the roar of the torrents nearly drove all of them mad.

As for Piskaret, since Menana could not marry him on earth, she turned him into a water spirit and married him beneath the wild, cascading waters.

THE CYCLOPS THVNDERED TOWARDS THEM

THE SEA NYMPH
AND THE CYCLOPS

Greek

ONG ago, in ancient Greece, a Cyclops lived in an island cave. The Cyclops was a hideous monster. He had a hairy body as tall as a mountain, and in the middle of his forehead was one huge rolling eye.

For centuries, the Cyclops lived a lonely horrid life. Even the forest dropped all its leaves in fright when the monster lumbered about the island. No humans ever willingly went near him—and with good reason: When a sailing ship strayed near his cave, the Cyclops caught the sailors and ate them for breakfast.

But one day an astonishing thing happened to the Cyclops. He fell in love with a sea nymph. Her name was Galatea and she was the daughter of the sea god, Nereus. Galatea was a charming and mocking nymph who spent her day swimming with her mermaid sisters or playing with her friend, Acis. Acis, the son of Pan, was a beautiful sixteen-year-old youth whom Galatea loved very much.

As much as Galatea loved Acis, she despised the ugly Cyclops. The Cyclops, however, yearned for the sea nymph, and his love for her made his personality change. He became kinder and more tender. He lost his taste for human blood. Rather than try to capture the sailors who sailed near his shore, he waved to them cheerfully. But most amazing of all, the Cyclops even began to care about his appearance. He stared into pools of water, searching for his reflection. He tried to comb his shaggy hair and cut his bushy beard.

The Cyclops' only friends were his flock of sheep. One day they followed him about the island as he searched for Galatea. Carrying a pine stick as tall as a ship's mast, he tramped along the shore. When his enormous feet grew tired, he sat on a rocky peninsula that jutted into the sea. As the waves splashed the gray rocks, the Cyclops played his homemade reed pipe. His music was so loud and hideous it made the mountains and waves tremble.

Little did the Cyclops know that Galatea and Acis were nearby embracing behind a rock. The Cyclops began to sing a love song.

> *O Galatea, more lovely than the winter sun,*
> *Sweeter than autumn grapes,*
> *Softer than a swan's down . . .*

The Cyclops heard laughter. He stopped singing and listened. After a moment of silence, he began again:

> *O Galatea, I'll give you anything.*
> *Every grape, every strawberry,*
> *All the little deer, rabbits, and bear cubs*
> *You can have them for toys.*

The Cyclops heard more laughter. He stopped singing and his one eye rolled suspiciously as he searched the shore. After a moment of silence, he began singing again:

> *O Galatea,*
> *I've looked at myself in the pool water.*
> *The more I looked, the more I liked what I saw.*

More laughter! The Cyclops was starting to get angry. He stood up and sang in a booming voice:

O Galatea, more stubborn than a cow.
Harder than an oak,
Vainer than a peacock,
Meaner than a snake . . .

Again, the Cyclops heard mocking laughter. He shook his walking stick at the sky and roared:

Galatea, listen to me!
Do you know who I am?
I own this island!
Each cave is mine! Each tree!

The Cyclops charged onto the shore. Huffing and puffing, he tramped all over the island, searching for the sea nymph. He lumbered over pastures and through woodlands.

The frightened couple tried to hide under a heap of rocks on the shore, but the Cyclops finally tracked them down. He glared at them with his huge rolling eye, and bellowed at Galatea, "I see you with him! But this is the last time you will ever be together!" His voice was so loud it shook Mt. Aetna with its echoes.

As the Cyclops thundered towards them, the sea nymph escaped by diving into the sea. But Acis was not a sea-born creature. He had no choice but to take off running. The Cyclops chased the boy along the shore. The monster tore a ton of rock from the mountain and hurled it at Acis. The giant rock buried the boy, killing him instantly.

When the Cyclops calmed down, he felt ashamed of murdering Acis. Furthermore, now he was certain he would never win the nymph, Galatea; so he hung his shaggy head and slouched away with his sheep.

Once the Cyclops was gone, Galatea crept out of the sea. When she realized what had happened to Acis, she screamed and fell to the ground. As she mourned the loss of her beloved, she regretted taunting the Cyclops. She asked the gods to forgive her for using her charms unwisely.

As if in answer to Galatea's prayer, blood flowed from the rock that had crushed Acis. Then melted snow and spring rains streamed out.

The blood, snow, and rain all ran together until the mighty boulder cracked, and a river raged forth. Then an even greater miracle occurred: A boy, as blue as the sea and as tall as a giant, stood waist-high in the flowing river. The boy was Acis; and from that day on, he was a mighty river god.

THE MERMAID OF GOLLERUS

He was living on the sunny side of life.

THE ENCHANTED CAP

Irish

NE fine summer day, Dick Fitzgerald stood on the shore of Gollerus, a village in the south of Ireland. The sun was rising behind the hills. The dark sea was turning green in the early light. The rolling mist curled up from the water like the smoke rising from Dick's pipe.

"What a pretty morning," said Dick. "Tis mighty lonesome to be talking to one's self, though. What in the wide world is a man without a wife? Why, he's no more complete than half a pair of scissors—or a fishing line without a hook."

Dick cast his eyes about. And what did he see, but a strange young woman sunning on a nearby rock. The morning light shone on her sea-green hair like melted butter shines on cabbage.

Dick guessed the truth. She was a mermaid. He spied her little enchanted red cap beside her—the sea people use enchanted caps for diving down deep into the ocean.

Dick Fitzgerald seized the little red cap, for he had once heard that if he could possess a mermaid's cap, she would lose the power to swim back home.

When the mermaid saw her cap was gone, she began to cry like a newborn babe. Salt tears—double salt, no doubt—came streaming down her face.

Though Dick knew quite well what ailed her, he could not help but feel sad. He did have a tender heart, after all. "Don't cry, my dear," he said.

But the mermaid only cried more.

Dick sat down on the rock and took her hand. He noticed it was not an ugly hand, in spite of the fact that there was a small web between her fingers, like that on a duck's foot. Her skin was as thin and white as the skin between the egg and its shell.

"What's your name?" said Dick.

She gave him no answer.

Dick squeezed her hand—for that's a universal language, you know. There's not a creature in the world does not understand it, fish or human.

The mermaid stopped weeping. "Man, will you now cook me for supper?" she said to Dick.

"By all check aprons between Dingle and Tralee!" said Dick. "I'd as soon cook and eat myself, my dear."

"Man," said the mermaid, "what will you do with me if you don't cook me for supper?"

Since Dick had been wanting a wife, he studied her hard. She was handsome, and she spoke like any real person. Yes, he decided he was fairly in love with her.

"Man, what will you do?" she asked again.

The way she called him "man" settled the matter entirely. "Fish," said Dick, trying to speak to her in her own fashion. "Fish, here's a word for you this blessed morning. I'll make you Mistress Fitzgerald before all the world. That's what I'll do with you."

"I'm ready and willing, Mister Fitzgerald," she said, "but first let me put my hair up."

After she fixed her hair, the mermaid stuck her comb in Dick's pocket. Then she bent her head close to the sea and whispered mysterious words to the water. Dick saw the murmuring of her words ripple on top of the waves. They slid towards the wide ocean like a breath of wind.

"Are you speaking to the water?" he asked in wonder.

"Just sending word home to my father," she said. "I'm telling him to go ahead and have his breakfast, not to wait for me."

"And who's your father, duck?" said Dick.

"He's the king of the waves," said the mermaid.

"Oh my!" said Dick. "You yourself must be a king's daughter then. To be sure, your father must have all the money that's down at the bottom of the sea."

"Money? What's money?" said the mermaid.

"Oh, tis not a bad thing," said Dick. "Maybe the fishes will bring some up."

"Yes, the fishes will bring me anything I want," she said.

"Oh, then speak to them," said Dick. "Tis only a straw bed I have at home. Not fit for a king's daughter. Maybe you'd like a nice feather bed. A pair of beds?"

"By all means, Mr. Fitzgerald, I have plenty of beds," she said. "Fourteen oyster beds of my own."

Dick scratched his head. He looked a bit puzzled. "That clearly is a nice thing to have," he said. "Nice to have one's bed so close to one's supper."

So Dick Fitzgerald took the mermaid to Father Fitzgibbon and asked him to marry them.

But the priest was appalled. "It is a fish woman you want to marry!" he shouted. "Send the scaly creature home to her own kind!"

"Please, father, she's a king's daughter," said Dick.

"Don't care if she's the daughter of fifty kings," said the priest. "She's a fish!"

"No, no, she's as mild and as beautiful as the moon," said Dick.

"I don't care if she's as mild and as beautiful as the moon, the sun, and the stars put together! You can't marry a fish, Dick! She's a fish—a fish!"

"But she has all the gold under the sea," said Dick.

"Oh. Oh. Well," said the priest. He straightened up. "That changes things entirely. Why didn't you tell me this before, Dick? Marry her for heaven's sake, even if she's ten times a fish."

So the priest married Dick and the mermaid. And everything prospered for old Dick. He was living on the sunny side of life, so to speak. The mermaid was the best of wives. The two lived very happily together and she promptly gave him three children besides.

In short, Dick Fitzgerald was a happy man, you could say. And he might have remained one to the end of his days, if he hadn't gone to Tralee on business one morning.

No sooner had Dick left the house than Mrs. Fitzgerald set about cleaning the place. Soon she chanced to come across some fishing tackle. And what do you think she found with it?

Yes. The enchanted red cap. The very one Dick stole the day they met long ago.

Mrs. Fitzgerald sat down on a little stool and just stared at the red cap. She thought about all the happy days she'd spent above the sea. She looked at her three human children, and she thought of poor Dick.

Oh, how it would break all their hearts to lose me, she thought sadly. *But they won't lose me entirely.* "I'll come back soon," she told them and kissed them each good-bye. "Who can blame me for going home for a bit of a visit?"

When Mrs. Fitzgerald put on her enchanted cap, she heard a faint singing coming from the sea, a strange, sweet song urging her to return to the land-under-the-waves from where she was stolen. And as she was suddenly flooded with memories of her father, the sea king; her mother, the sea queen; and of her sea brothers and sisters; she felt a great longing to be with all of them again.

So Mrs. Fitzgerald rushed to the shore of Gollerus where the sea was calm and smooth and glittering in the sunlight. As she plunged into the water and disappeared, her human family was quickly forgotten.

When Dick came home that evening, his daughter told him about her mother's departure. Dick rushed to his fishing tackle and looked for the enchanted cap. When he saw it was gone, he was certain of the truth.

Year after year, Dick Fitzgerald waited for his mermaid wife to come back home. He never married again. And to his dying day, nothing persuaded him she would not have returned if she could have.

"Her father, the king, must have kept her in the sea by force," were Dick's very last words.

All others seemed to agree with Dick. Until this day in that part of Ireland, the "Mermaid of Gollerus" is spoken of as the very model of a perfect wife and mother.

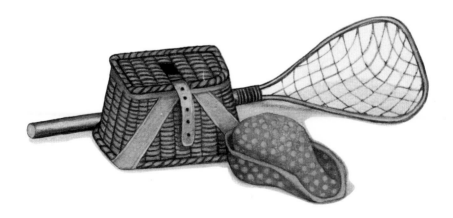

"YOU MUST DO ONE MORE THING."

NASTASIA OF THE SEA

Ukrainian

LONG ago, a man and his wife went to work in a wheat field in Ukraine. They took their baby boy with them and laid him down in the grass. No sooner had they started to cut the wheat than an eagle swooped from the sky and stole the baby.

The eagle carried the boy to his nest. He named him Tremsin and took good care of him for many years. But on Tremsin's sixteenth birthday, the eagle said, "Now you must go out into the world and find your own way."

Before Tremsin could object, the eagle kicked him out of the nest. When Tremsin landed on the ground, he was quite frightened. Having no idea how to find his own way, he hung his head and wept.

"What's wrong?" said a voice.

Tremsin looked up and saw a horse. "I don't know what to do!" cried Tremsin. "How will I ever find my way in the world?"

"I don't know," said the horse. "But I do have one piece of advice: If you ever come across a feather of the Burning Bright Bird, do not pick it up, or you will get into great trouble."

Tremsin and the horse traveled on through the Ukrainian countryside until one day they came across a shining feather, lying in their path. "Remember what I said," warned the horse.

But Tremsin ignored the wise animal, and he picked up the feather of the Burning Bright Bird. Then he rode on until he came to the estate of a rich nobleman. Tremsin asked the nobleman for work and was given a job in the stables. Whenever he brushed the nobleman's horses with the feather of the Burning Bright Bird, Tremsin made their coats shine like burnished silver.

The other stable boys grew quite jealous of Tremsin, so they plotted to get rid of him. They went to the nobleman and said, "Tremsin has a feather of the Burning Bright Bird. He swears he can get the bird herself for you."

"Ah, bring Tremsin to me," said the nobleman. He greedily rubbed his hands together, for the Burning Bright Bird was the rarest bird in all of Ukraine.

When Tremsin came before him, the nobleman said, "I order you to capture the Burning Bright Bird and bring her to me."

"Oh, sir, I cannot," said Tremsin.

"Do it, or I'll cut off your head," said the nobleman.

"I'll try," said Tremsin.

But alone with his horse, he wept. "I cannot do this impossible task."

"This is not a big task, Tremsin," his horse said. "'Tis a mere trifle. Strip yourself naked and lie in the grass. When the Burning Bright Bird swoops down to peck out your eye, seize her by the leg."

So Tremsin went to the wild steppes and flung himself naked onto the high grass. At noon, when the Burning Bright Bird swooped down to peck out his eye, he seized her by the leg. Then he threw on his clothes and carried her to the nobleman, and the nobleman rewarded him with great praise.

After Tremsin's feat, the stable boys grew even more envious. They plotted again to get rid of Tremsin. One of them said to the nobleman, "Tremsin brought you the Burning Bright Bird. Now he says he can get the thrice-lovely Nastasia of the sea."

"Ah, bring Tremsin to me," said the nobleman. He rubbed his hands together, for the thrice-lovely Nastasia was the most astonishing water maid in all the land.

"Tremsin," said the nobleman, "I bid you to capture the thrice-lovely Nastasia and bring her to me."

"Oh no, sir! I cannot," said Tremsin.

"Do it, or I'll cut off your head."

"I'll try," said Tremsin. But as soon as he left the nobleman, he burst into tears.

"Why do you weep?" said his faithful horse.

"This task will surely kill me," said Tremsin. "I have no idea how to fetch the thrice-lovely Nastasia from the sea."

"This is not a big task, Tremsin," said his horse. "'Tis a mere trifle. Do this: Set up a white tent by the shore. Fill it with lovely things. Then wait for the thrice-lovely Nastasia to come out of the sea."

Tremsin set up the white tent. He filled it with beautiful scarves, trinkets, fruits, and wine.

Soon the thrice-lovely Nastasia emerged from the sea. She tried on the scarves and trinkets. She ate the fruit and drank the wine. Then she lay down in the tent and closed her eyes.

Tremsin could hardly believe his great fortune. No sooner had Nastasia fallen asleep than he crept into the tent and seized her. Then he carried her on horseback to the nobleman.

The nobleman was so pleased that he allowed Tremsin to keep Nastasia.

But the water maid could not be so easily won. She spoke sharply to Tremsin: "You have captured me, but you have not captured my love. If you wish to capture that, you must find my coral necklace in the sea."

"Oh, but that is an impossible task!" cried Tremsin. His heart nearly broke, for by now he was deeply in love with the thrice-lovely Nastasia. He'd never before met such a bold and remarkable maiden.

"Tis not an impossible task," said Tremsin's faithful horse, "but a mere trifle. Watch for a crab to come from the water. Then say, 'I'll catch thee!'"

Tremsin went to the sea. When a crab crawled out from the waves, he shouted, "I'll catch thee!"

"Please don't!" said the crab. "If you let me return to the sea, I'll help you. I promise to get you anything you need."

"Ah," said Tremsin, "fetch me the coral necklace of the thrice-lovely Nastasia."

The crab called her children together and said, "Collect all the coral under the waves and bring it ashore."

When the tiniest crab dragged Nastasia's coral necklace from the ocean's depth, Tremsin cheered. Then he mounted his steed and hurried to Nastasia.

"Your necklace!" he said, proudly presenting it to her.

"Thank you," said Nastasia a bit haughtily. "You've captured me, and you've captured my necklace. But if you wish to capture my love, you must gather my herd of wild horses from the sea."

"Oh, but that is an impossible task!" said Tremsin. His heart nearly broke. By now he was more deeply in love with Nastasia than ever. He'd never before met such a bold and remarkable maiden.

This time Tremsin's horse grieved also. "Tis not a mere trifle, but an enormous task," he told Tremsin. "For the thrice-lovely Nastasia has a thrice-terrible mare."

"Please don't tell me that," said Tremsin.

"Then let me think." His horse thought for a moment, then said, "Do this. Buy twenty animal hides and load them on my back. Carry a whip and lead me to the sea."

Tremsin loaded his horse with twenty animal hides; then he led him to the sea.

"Now, I will plunge into the water," said the horse. "Wait until you see the thrice-terrible mare swimming behind me. Then strike her on the forehead with your whip."

Tremsin's horse plunged into the water. He swam out to the waves where Nastasia's sea horses were grazing. Suddenly Nastasia's thrice-terrible mare saw Tremsin's horse. With great fury, the mare and the rest of the herd chased after the steed.

When the mare caught up with Tremsin's horse, she tried to bite him. But instead, she ripped one of the animal hides off his back and tore it to shreds. She caught him a second time. But again, she ripped off another hide and tore it to shreds.

This happened twenty times and for seventy leagues across the sea.

Finally Tremsin saw his horse coming in on a large, billowing wave. Behind his faithful horse galloped the thrice-lovely Nastasia's thrice-terrible mare and her thrice-terrible herd.

Tremsin waded into the water. He cracked his whip and struck the mare on her forehead.

She instantly came to a stop.

Tremsin threw a halter over her. He mounted her and drove the whole herd out of the water.

"Your wild horses!" he said, proudly presenting them to the thrice-lovely Nastasia.

"Thank you," she said a bit haughtily. "You've captured me, and you've captured my coral necklace and my horses. But before you capture my love, you must do one more thing."

"What? Anything! Anything!" said Tremsin.

"Milk my mare and put her milk into three barrels. In the first barrel, the milk must be boiling hot. In the second, it must be lukewarm. In the third, it must be icy cold."

"Oh, but that is an impossible task!" said Tremsin. His heart nearly broke, for by now he was deliriously in love with the thrice-lovely Nastasia. He had never before met such a bold and remarkable maiden.

"Gather your courage, Tremsin," scolded his horse. "And just do as she says."

Tremsin did as the thrice-lovely Nastasia ordered.

When all the barrels were ready, she said, "Now leap in and out of each barrel of milk."

Tremsin leapt into the boiling hot barrel. When he leapt out, he was an old man.

He leapt into the lukewarm barrel. When he leapt out, he was a little boy.

He leapt into the icy cold barrel. When he leapt out, he was more handsome and goodly than words can describe.

The thrice-lovely Nastasia leapt in and out of each barrel. When she leapt out of the first, she was an old woman.

When she leapt out of the second, she was a little girl.

When she leapt out of the third, she was more handsome and goodly than words can describe.

Finally, the thrice-lovely Nastasia took Tremsin for her husband. They and their horses lived half of the year under the sea and half of the year on the Ukrainian steppes. In both lands, they lived happily ever after.

THE FISH HUSBAND

Nigerian

ONG ago, in an African village, there lived a very beautiful girl. All the men in the village were bewitched by her, and asked for her hand in marriage. But steadfastly she refused. She insisted she would only marry the most handsome man in all the land.

One day, as the girl was browsing through the market place, she saw a very striking man, and instantly she fell in love with him.

Boldly, the beautiful girl approached the man. "Sir, I love you," she said. "If you will have me, I will be your wife."

"Oh, I should like very much to have you for my wife," he said, "but sadly, I cannot. For I am not a man and I am not of your people. I only look like a man because the gods have given me the power to turn into one whenever I visit land. But in truth, I am a fish and my true home is the river at Idunmaibo. And to the river I must return."

"I don't care if you're man or fish," the girl said, "I still love you. If you promise to come forth from the water from time to time to visit me, I will still gladly marry you."

"Then let it be so. Come with me," said the fish man, and he led the girl to a certain place on the river at Idunmaibo where they were married.

Then the fish man spoke again to the girl. "This is my home," he said. "Whenever you want me, come to this very place and sing a magic song." Then the fish man sang a lovely song:

> *Oh beautiful fish of the river,*
> *May I look through the flowing waters?*
> *Through the surface of the river I will see you.*
> *Oh lovely river that looks like silver and gems*
> *With palace beneath, more lovely*
> *Than the palace of kings of men.*

The fish man then dove into the water and disappeared from sight.

Every day thereafter, the girl prepared sweetmeats for her husband and carried them to Idunmaibo. There, by the river, she sang the magic song, and the fish came to the surface and changed into a handsome man.

The fish man gave the girl many gifts—beautiful coral and gems of the sea—and he sat with her on the river bank, and they both loved each other very much.

One day, while the girl was making a basket of sweetmeats, her parents told her she must get married soon. The girl replied that she already had a husband, but she could not tell them who he was.

Her family was indeed very puzzled by her answer, and they watched her closely as she prepared her husband's food. Her brother asked if he might help her carry it. But she told him she must go alone and nobody must follow her. This only aroused her brother's curiosity, and he made up his mind to follow her to see where she went and what she did with the food. Using magic, he turned himself into a fly. Then he flew behind his sister all the way to Idunmaibo. There the fly brother watched the girl as she sang her magic song. To his astonishment, he saw the fish come out of the water and turn into a man. And he saw the fish man visit with his sister, then jump back into the water.

The girl's brother quickly flew back home. He changed from a fly back into a boy and hastened to his parents to tell them what he had seen.

The girl's parents were enraged when they heard about the fish man. They decided to send their daughter away until they could figure out what to do. So as soon as the girl returned from the river at Idunmaibo, her parents sent her to live with her father's people—far, far from the river.

The poor girl was heartbroken because she could no longer visit the fish man. While she was away grieving, her brother led her father to the river at Idunmaibo. There, the brother sang the magic song, and the fish man rose from the water.

As soon as the fish man stepped onto the bank of the river, the girl's father drew a long knife and stabbed him. The handsome young man was mortally wounded and, as he died, he slowly shriveled into a fish, then disappeared.

Soon after, the girl was sent home from her relatives. She could hardly wait to rush back to the river and into the arms of her beloved. She quickly prepared the fish man's meal, and was in such a hurry that she hadn't noticed her brother following close behind her.

The girl stood on the bank and sang her lovely magic song, but the fish man did not rise from the river. She waited a moment, then sang her song again, but still the fish man did not appear.

Suddenly, she heard someone singing the magic song. Filled with hope, she turned around, expecting to find the fish man, but was startled to find her brother.

"He will come to you no longer," her brother told her, "for our father has slain him."

Toda trembled when he saw her.

THE SER-PENT AND THE SEA QUEEN

THE SERPENT
AND THE SEA QUEEN

Japanese

ONG ago in the land of Japan, an earthquake created a small emerald-green island. Surrounding the island was the World-Under-the-Sea. This world was ruled by the Sea King and Sea Queen. They lived in a palace made of shells, coral, marble, and precious gems; and all the creatures of the sea were their servants.

The Sea King ruled the tides. He sent rains and floods. He breathed the wind and lashed the waves into foam. Never did the Sea King leave the sea. But the Sea Queen enjoyed visiting the island. She rode a mighty green dragon through the water until she arrived on land. Then she disguised herself as one of the ladies of the emperor's court by donning red and white robes.

One year the Sea Queen built a summer palace on the island shore. She planted beautiful gardens, grain fields, and mulberry plantations. But it wasn't long before a hideous monster attacked her land.

The monster was a great serpent named Ja. Ja had a mustache made of snakes, and he had one million legs. His eyes blazed with fire, and his body was so long he could coil it seven times around the mountain of Mikami.

One day when the Sea Queen was gone, Ja ate all her fruit and grain. He tore into her palace and ate her servants, too. He swallowed them all in one gulp, then spat out their bones.

When the Sea Queen returned to her palace, she began screaming in horror. She rushed out into the fields, screaming and tearing her hair. "Can no one destroy the terrible Ja?" she cried out.

At that moment, a young warrior named Toda the Archer was passing by. When Toda saw the distraught woman, he did not realize she was the Sea Queen.

"How can I help you, poor lady?" he asked.

"Slay Ja for me!" the Sea Queen cried. "He has destroyed my home!"

"I will do as you wish," said Toda the Archer. And he set out across the island.

While he looked for Ja, Toda planned his attack. He knew the only thing that could kill the horrible serpent was human saliva. If he moistened the tip of his arrow and struck Ja, the creature would die at once.

As night fell, Toda crept over a small bridge with his bow in his hand. He could see nothing in the twilight except mist rising from the lake. But suddenly two flames shot into the sky. Ja's head plunged through the mist! His mustache writhed with thousands of snakes!

Toda rushed back across the bridge. He shot at the horrid monster. But Toda was so fearful he forgot to wet his arrow; so when the arrow hit Ja, it did not even wound him. The serpent roared with fury; the mountains echoed and the earth trembled. Ja's eyes flamed with rage as he began slithering across the bridge towards Toda.

But Toda held his ground. As he started to aim again at the monster, he remembered he must wet his arrow tip with saliva. He quickly did so, then shot the arrow directly into Ja's forehead.

The monster howled and roared. As he flung back his head, his mustache writhed and rattled. Then slowly all the horrible snakes began to die. When they hung limply from Ja's face, the monster's long body jerked about, then stiffened. Finally, Ja was dead.

Out of the dark night the Sea Queen came riding. Toda trembled when he saw her on the back of her mighty green dragon. "Who are you?" he called out, shielding his eyes from her brightness.

"I am the Sea Queen," she said. "It was I who begged you to slay the terrible Ja. And though you did not know who I was, you risked your life for me."

Toda was so surprised he could not speak.

"Now I wish to reward your kindness and courage," said the Sea Queen. "Come with me to my palace in the World-Under-the-Sea."

The Sea Queen clapped her hands, and instantly, a boat made of shells rose from the depths of the water.

The Sea Queen beckoned Toda to climb into the boat. When her green dragon plunged into the sea, Toda's boat followed him down into the deepest waters.

Finally the Sea Queen and Toda arrived in the heart of the World-Under-the-Sea. Toda could not believe his eyes. Light was pouring through the water, shining upon a glittering palace. Gardens of seaweeds bloomed everywhere.

But most enchanting of all were the hundreds of sea fairies that danced around Toda's boat. The fairies wore robes of shells fringed with mother-of-pearl. On their heads were headdresses made of living sea creatures—crabs, lobsters, squid, seahorses, clams, and shrimps. As the fairies danced around Toda, their headdresses waved their legs and tails, clacked their shells, and twirled their feelers.

When the dance ended, the Sea Queen turned to Toda. "In honor of your great courage, I would like to present you with these gifts," she said.

The sea fairies then filled Toda's boat with huge casks of rice, jars of wine, silk robes, a mighty sword, and a huge bronze bell.

Then the Sea Queen kissed Toda good-bye. "Thank you," she said. "Farewell."

The sea fairies escorted Toda to the edge of the World-Under-the-Sea. Then his boat rose out of the depths of the deep water and returned to the island shore.

When Toda stepped out of the boat, his frantic servants rushed forward to greet him. They'd been searching for him everywhere. Toda tried to explain where he'd been, but when he turned back to the boat, he saw it was gone. All of his gifts, however, were piled on the sand.

Over the years, Toda discovered many wondrous things about the Sea Queen's gifts. Her casks of rice never became empty. Her jars of wine always brimmed over. Her silk robes never wore out, and her mighty sword conquered all whom it touched.

Long after Toda and his descendants died, the Sea Queen's bronze bell hung in a temple near the lake. As it swung in the night breeze, its mellow notes rolled over the lake and echoed in the mountains.

Even today, the great bell wakes the white herons, the monks, and the mulberry pickers who live on the island. Whenever the bell sounds, if one gazes into the depths of the lake, one might catch a glimpse of the Sea Queen's glittering palace.

Ȳ TIDE WAS RISING.

THE MERMAID'S REVENGE
English

ONG ago, in Cornwall, a farmer and his wife lived in a humble mud cottage. But they had a lovely garden, a good life, and a beautiful daughter named Selina.

Selina had rosy cheeks and dark, mysterious eyes. The gossips in the village said that long ago Selina's mother had taken her to the Pool of Perran, a favorite haunt of mermaids. Little Selina had leapt from her mother's arms into the water. When she reappeared, her face was more bright and enchanting than ever.

One night in her eighteenth year, Selina was walking on the seashore with her father. As the cold clear moon flooded the ocean with light, a young soldier rode by. His name was Walter Trewoofe, and he was visiting his uncle, a wealthy squire.

Selina thought Walter was quite elegant and striking on the back of his proud horse. Likewise, when Walter observed Selina and her father, he was struck by the quiet beauty of the girl.

Thereafter, Walter schemed to ride his horse along the sands whenever Selina was strolling with her father. And whenever he passed them, he stopped to say something flattering to the girl.

Soon the lonely, beautiful maiden fell in love with Walter Trewoofe, and she began taking walks with him instead of with her father. Once when Walter and Selina were strolling along the shore, an old fisherman saw a strange sight: a mermaid rising from the depths of the sea. The mermaid floated along the billowing waves as if she were keeping watch over the young girl.

When Selina did not see Walter, the world seemed grey and cold; when she *did* see him, the world was filled with sunshine. But Walter did not have honorable intentions toward Selina. He was quite conceited; in fact, he expected all young maidens to fall in love with him. So after courting Selina for a short while, he grew bored and disappeared back into the busy world of London. Never did he even think of her feelings.

Back in the fishing village in Cornwall, Selina mourned for Walter Trewoofe. She lay in her bed and slowly faded from this life. As she grew weaker, everything went wrong in the village. Crops failed, haystacks and corn ricks caught fire. Horses fell lame. And cows died.

Finally one night, at the moment the tide turned and the waters of the sea began to recede from the shore, Selina slipped from life into death.

That same night, by coincidence, Walter Trewoofe had returned to Cornwall to visit his uncle, the squire. Walter attended a grand party near the coast. At midnight, he left the party and wandered along the edge of the cliffs. Soon he stumbled down to the beach. He was lost, so he began to retrace his steps. But then the most exquisite music stopped him.

Walter heard a woman singing a forlorn and melancholy song:

> *Come away, come away*
> *O'er the waters wild*
> *Our earth-born child*
> *Died this day, died this day.*

Walter walked slowly along the sands. He discovered the sweet sounds were coming from the low waters, on the other side of the rocks. At the mouth of a cavern he saw a woman who looked exactly like Selina.

She stared up at the stars and sang her song:

> *Come away, come away*
> *The tempest proud*
> *Weaves the shroud*
> *For him who did betray.*

Walter began walking through the low waters until he came to the woman. She extended her arms as if to welcome him. "Come, sit beside me, Walter," she said in a beautiful, silvery voice.

Walter sat beside her, and she wreathed her arms around his neck and looked into his eyes.

"Kisses are as true at sea as they are false on land," she said. "You kiss a maiden, then betray her. But if a sea maiden kisses you, you will be hers forever." And she kissed him.

Walter realized that this was not Selina.

As if she had read his mind, the woman said, "I am Selina's mermaid guardian. I have been watching over her since she fell into the Pool of Perran as a small child. Now I avenge her death."

Walter began to struggle with the mermaid. But she held him tightly. The tide was rising and the winds roared. Lightning struck. Then a black mist covered the star-filled sky.

As the waves crashed against the shore, the mermaid pulled Walter to a higher rock. The thunder boomed above the iron cliffs. Then a mighty wave splashed against the highest rock, and Walter and the mermaid were carried out to sea.

As they floated through the water, the mermaid held Walter by his hair. And she sang in a voice as clear as a bell:

Come away, come away
The tempest proud
Weaves the shroud
For him who did betray.

Walter heard other voices singing above the roar of the storm. A chorus of silvery voices sang:

Come away, come away
Beneath the wave
Lieth the grave
Of him we slay, him we slay.

Then Selina's mermaid guardian bore Walter Trewoofe down under the waves.

THE PRIN-CESS OF THE TUNG LAKE

THE PRINCESS
OF THE TUNG LAKE

Chinese

ONG ago in ancient China, a general was fishing on the Tung Lake. When he spied a huge fish swimming beneath the surface of the lake, he shot an arrow and wounded the creature in the back.

The fish was pulled out of the water and attached to the mast of the ship. But the general's servant, a young man named Chen Pichiao, could not bear to watch the fish dangle helplessly in the air.

"There is something about this fish that fills my heart with sympathy," he said to the general. "May I please put it back in the water?"

Chen persisted until finally the general agreed to let the fish go. Chen was so concerned about the fish he even put a piece of plaster on its wound before lowering it back into the Tung Lake.

A year later, Chen was crossing the Tung Lake alone, and his small boat was caught in a sudden squall. As the boat began to sink, Chen saved himself by clinging to a bamboo crate. After drifting all night, he caught an overhanging tree branch and scrambled onto the shore.

Exhausted from his ordeal, he rested on the lake shore, beneath

home. He often told his relatives and his friends about his adventures with the princess of the Tung Lake. Though everyone enjoyed his stories, no one really believed them.

But then one day a man from Chen's village named Liang was crossing the Tung Lake. Suddenly Liang saw an ornamental barge with carved woodwork and red windows. He heard music and singing. When he peeked into the barge he saw none other than his friend Chen sitting with the lake princess.

"Chen! It is you!" said Liang.

"Why are you so surprised, friend?" said Chen. "I have been telling everyone all along about my life on the Tung Lake."

"But—but—" sputtered Liang.

"Won't you join us for wine and food?" said the princess.

Liang visited several hours with Chen and the lake princess. "I must be on my way, now," he said.

"Please say hello to my wife and family," said Chen.

"Indeed," said Liang, a bit dazed. "This news will surprise them all, I'm sure."

Liang said good-bye and headed for home.

But as soon as Liang stepped foot in his own village, whom should he see but Chen! Drinking with a party of friends in the local tea house!

"How did you get back home before me?" cried Liang.

"I don't know what you mean," said Chen. "I have been here all day."

"No you haven't!" said Liang. "I saw you on the lake with the princess!"

"You are mistaken. Chen has been here all day with us," said one of Chen's friends.

"Indeed he has," said another.

"No! No! He can't be in two places at once!" Liang shouted.

As Liang kept ranting and raving, everyone only laughed and told him he was crazy.

After many years of a long and happy life, Chen passed away at the age of eighty. When his coffin bearers carried his coffin to its grave, they thought it was remarkably light. They opened it, and found his body had disappeared. In its place was a bit of seaweed and some water. The coffin bearers gasped in astonishment.

"The lake princess must have worked her final magic," whispered Liang.

THE SEA PRINCESS
OF PERSIA

Iranian

ONG, long ago a king of Persia had a hundred wives, but none had given him a child. One day a servant rushed into the king's chambers. "Your majesty," he cried, "there's a merchant at the door with an enchanting slave girl!"

"Let them in," said the king.

The merchant brought in the slave girl. When he removed a blue silk veil from her face, the king's chambers seemed lit by a thousand torches. The girl's hair fell down her back in seven heavy braids that touched her ankles; her eyes were so bright they would heal the sick.

"Praise Allah!" said the king. He gave the merchant ten thousand gold coins in exchange for the slave. Then he sent the merchant away. "Please tell me your name," he said to the girl. "And tell me the name of your native land."

The slave girl did not look at the king, nor speak. She only stared sorrowfully into the distance.

A fire burned in the king's heart. He desperately wanted to win the love of the sad girl.

"We must mend her broken heart," he told his servants. "Treat her with great honor. Anoint her with scents and give her the palace room with the windows overlooking the sea."

At the mention of the sea, the girl lifted her eyes and a faint smile flickered across her face.

The servants took her to her palace room and treated her with great kindness. And each day the king visited her and tried to win her trust. "Please, tell me your name," he said, "and tell me the name of your native land."

But the girl always remained silent.

Day after day, the fire in the king's heart burned brighter and brighter. He thought of nothing but how to win the slave girl's love. He called together all the singers in the kingdom and ordered them to sing music for the sad girl.

The singers sang wonderful songs; they delighted everyone, except the girl. She sat alone, unmoved, her head lowered, her heart broken.

Next the king sent for all the dancers in his kingdom and ordered them to dance for the sad girl.

The dancers danced for many hours; they delighted everyone, except the girl. She sat alone, unmoved, her head lowered, her heart broken.

Soon the king's heart began to break also. "Please," he begged the girl one day, "you must tell me what you want. I will give you anything."

It was no use. The slave girl would neither look at him nor speak to him.

Finally the king could bear it no longer. "Heart of my heart," he said to the slave girl, "do you not know that I love you? For weeks I have borne your silence and your coldness, and now I fear I will soon die of grief."

The girl slowly raised her eyes. "Great-hearted king," she said.

"I swore never to speak again, but your kindness has softened my resolve. I've kept silent because I am angry about being a slave. I miss my mother, my brother, and the land of my birth."

"Praise Allah!" said the king. "You have spoken your heart! Now tell me about your land and your people! What is your name? How did you come to be a slave?"

"My name is Princess Julnare. My land is the Land-Under-the-Sea. My people are the children of the sea. One night I left my home in the waters and climbed to the shore for a visit. In the moonlight, the warm breeze wooed me to sleep. When I woke, a slave merchant had captured me."

The king took the girl's hands in his own. "Princess Julnare," he said, "please forgive the ways of men."

"I do forgive them—because of you," she said. "And because your kindness is so great, I will give you a child."

The king felt lifted from the very earth by his joy. He hurried out to his people to spread the good news. He gave a hundred thousand gold coins to the poor as a token of his gratitude to Allah.

The next year a plump, rosy-faced boy was born to Princess Julnare. The prince shone with the brightness of the full moon.

When the king saw his son, his joy knew no bounds. He ordered seven days of celebration, and during those days he gave gifts to the poor and released all prisoners and freed all his slaves.

On the eighth day, Princess Julnare named her son Smile-of-the-Moon. After the naming ceremony, she drew her husband to her. "I will not be completely free of sorrow until I see my family again," she said. "I beg you to allow me to send for my mother, Queen Locust of the Sea, and my brother, the Prince of the Sea. I want them to bless our child."

"Of course!" said the king. "But how do I bring your family from the sea?"

"I will do it," she said. "You may go in the next room and watch."

The king hid in the next room and watched his wife place two pieces of sweet-smelling wood upon a fire. When the smoke began to rise, she whistled, then murmured strange magic words.

At once, the sea opened. Out of its depths rose a handsome youth with rose-colored cheeks and sea-green hair. Next rose an old woman with white hair and a ruby crown.

The two sea people walked upon the surface of the water until they came to the palace. Then they leapt upwards—as light as foam—and flew through the window to Princess Julnare and kissed her with tears of great joy.

The princess took her baby boy and placed him in the arms of his uncle. The prince lifted the baby high into the air, kissed him a thousand times, and bounced him up and down.

Then as the king watched from his hiding place, he saw a terrible sight: The prince suddenly leapt through the window with the tiny baby, and he disappeared down into the sea!

The king screamed in horror. He flew into the next room. "My son! My son!" he cried. "I've lost my son!"

"Wait," whispered Princess Julnare. She pointed at the waves out her window.

They parted. The sea opened. And the prince emerged with Smile-of-the-Moon in his arms.

The young prince leapt from the sea through the palace window, and the king saw that his son was sleeping peacefully in his uncle's arms. In fact, the baby was smiling like the moon itself.

"Oh, King, were you frightened when I jumped into the sea with this small one?" said the prince.

"Yes, uncle of my son," said the king. "I despaired he would drown and I would never ever see him again."

The prince smiled. "From now on, you need never fear your son might drown," he said. "For the rest of his life he'll be able to leap into the sea without harm. I have given him the same birthright as all the children of the sea."

The prince handed the boy to the king. Then he drew a cloth bag from his belt and poured its contents upon the carpet.

The king gasped. Before him were pearls the size of pigeons' eggs and the thousand fires of a thousand underwater jewels. The room was ablaze with the sort of fantastic lights one only sees in dreams.

"My mother and I must depart now," said the Prince of the Sea. "We yearn for our native land."

Princess Julnare bid her mother and brother a tearful good-bye. They promised to return from time to time. Then they leapt through the window and disappeared below the ocean waters.

From that day on, the Sea Princess of Persia lived happily with the King of Persia. And their little Smile-of-the-Moon grew up to be very brave and very wise.

THE MERMAID
IN THE MILLPOND

German

 ONG ago a miller and his wife lived in the Black Forest. They had plenty of land and plenty of money. But just as a thief comes in the night, ill luck crept into the miller's life, and his good fortune began to wane until he'd lost almost everything.

The poor miller was so distraught about his misfortune he could not eat or sleep. He wrung his hands and paced his floor at night. To add to his burdens, his wife told him that she would soon be having a baby.

One early morning, after a sleepless night of despair, the miller decided to drown himself in the millpond. "My wife will be better off if I die," he said, "for then she'll be free to marry someone who has better luck, who can take good care of her and our child."

Without even saying farewell to his wife, the miller crept out of their house and headed down to the millpond. In the gray light of dawn, he stood by the water and tried to gather the courage to drown himself.

But as the miller stared at the pond, the first sunbeam broke over its glassy surface, the water rippled, and a beautiful mermaid rose from the deep.

The miller was speechless; he stared in amazement at the mermaid.

She had long, dark wavy hair and eyes the color of the bluest water.

"Why are you so sad, dear miller?" she asked in a lovely voice.

The miller took heart to hear such a kind voice inquire after him. "Once I lived in great wealth," he said. "But now through no fault of my own I am poor."

"Oh, I will make you richer than ever before," said the mermaid. "But on one condition: You must give me your first child."

The miller was horrified. "Oh no, never!" he said.

"I promise your child will have a wonderful life with me," said the mermaid. "Besides, what are your choices? You must either give your baby to me or drown yourself in despair. No?"

The desperate miller could see no other solution to his problems, so he promised to exchange his first-born child for wealth and riches.

"You've decided wisely," said the mermaid. And with that, she disappeared into the depths of the millpond.

The miller was anxious about his promise to the mermaid. But by the time he got home, his tattered clothing had turned into the finest silk. His pockets were bulging with gold coins. And his humble cottage had changed into a castle.

When the miller went inside the castle, he was overjoyed to find his wife lying on a luxurious bed, dressed in the finest gown.

"Oh, our new baby boy has brought us great luck!" his wife cried. "No sooner did I give birth at dawn, than everything changed!"

"Our baby boy?" said the miller. He was astonished to discover his child had been born in his absence. As he looked at the beautiful infant, he burst into tears. He threw himself on the bed and told his wife about his terrible promise to the mermaid.

His wife was furious, of course. But she did not waste time yelling at him. Rather, she hugged her baby and said fiercely, "She will *never* have him! We will watch him every moment of his life and make sure he stays far away from the millpond!"

Just as the mermaid had promised, great prosperity flowed into the miller's life. But he did not keep his part of the bargain, for he and his wife *never* let their son go near the millpond.

"Beware!" they warned the boy constantly. "If you but touch the water, a hand will rise up and drag you down."

As the years passed, the miller and his wife worried less and less about their son. The boy always avoided the millpond, and the mermaid was not capable of traveling on land, so there seemed to be no way for her to capture him.

When the boy grew up, he became a brave huntsman. He married a kind maiden, and the two lived happily together in a beautiful cottage of their own.

But one day when the huntsman was chasing a deer, he pursued it into an open meadow that was crossed by a stream. Unbeknownst to the young man, the stream fed into the millpond.

Hot and thirsty from the chase, the huntsman fell to the ground and washed his face in the cool stream waters.

Suddenly the mermaid surfaced. Before the huntsman could escape, she wound her arms around his neck and dragged him down into the water.

The huntsman opened his mouth to scream, but water rushed down his throat. His nose and eyes filled with water and the world turned to black. Not even a ripple was left on the surface of the stream.

When the huntsman did not come home, his wife became alarmed. She hurried to the miller's castle and told the old couple about their son's disappearance. The miller and his wife explained about the terrible promise made long ago to the mermaid. They were too feeble to leave home, so they begged the girl to search for their son.

The huntsman's wife rushed down to the millpond. She walked around the pond until she discovered the small stream. She followed the stream into the open meadow, and there she found her husband's hunting pouch in the weeds.

The huntsman's wife walked around and around the millpond, calling her beloved's name. But the surface of the water stayed calm. As the moon shone down upon the girl, she sobbed softly. Several times she cried out, "Give him back to me! Give him back!"

But no answer greeted her.

At midnight, the exhausted girl sank to the ground and fell into a deep sleep.

While she slept, she dreamed she was climbing great rocks. Thorns and briars tore her feet and the wind tossed her hair. But finally she reached the summit of a mountain. There she found a green meadow filled with flowers. In the middle of the meadow stood a tiny cottage. An old woman opened the door and beckoned the girl inside.

"I'll help you," the old woman said. "Here is my golden comb. When you wake, comb your long hair."

When the girl woke up from her sleep, she found a golden comb in her hand, the same one the old woman had given her in her dream. "How can this mere comb bring him back?" she asked sorrowfully.

Nevertheless, she began combing her long hair with the comb. Suddenly a large wave rolled to the shore and, in the moonlight, the waters parted. Then the huntsman's head appeared! He looked at his wife and shouted with great joy, for he was so close to his freedom!

But as soon as he cried out, a second wave covered the huntsman. He vanished, leaving the millpond as still as before.

The girl wept with grief. For the rest of that night and all the next day she mourned by the pond.

Around midnight of the second night, the huntsman's wife fell into a deep sleep again, and soon she was climbing the mountain.

When she arrived at the tiny cottage, the old woman opened her door and said, "Take my golden flute. When you wake, play a beautiful song."

The girl woke and found herself holding the golden flute the old woman had given her in her dream. "How can a flute possibly bring him back?" she asked sorrowfully.

Nevertheless, the huntsman's wife began playing a hauntingly sweet tune. Suddenly a wave rolled to the shore and, in the moonlight, the waters parted.

This time, not only did the huntsman's head appear, but half his body rose out of the water. He reached towards his wife with a look of great yearning. But no sooner did his hands touch hers, than a second wave covered him again.

The girl wept with grief. For the rest of the night and all the next day she mourned by the millpond.

Around midnight of the third night, the huntsman's wife fell into a deep sleep, and again she dreamed she was climbing the mountain to the old woman's cottage.

This time when the old woman opened the door, the girl cried, "Alas! What good is it to keep seeing my beloved, only to lose him again?"

"Take my golden spinning wheel," said the old woman. "When the moon is high, sit near the shore and spin the spool full."

The huntsman's wife woke to find herself sitting next to a golden spinning wheel. "How can a spinning wheel possibly bring him back?" she asked sorrowfully.

But no sooner did the huntsman's wife begin to spin than a mighty wave swept across the moonlit millpond. This time, the whole body of her beloved rose into the air. And this time, he sprang to the shore!

Both of them shouted with great joy.

THE LITTLE MERMAID
Danish

ONCE upon a time, far out to sea, where the water was as blue as the petals of the loveliest cornflower, lived the Mer-king. Since the Mer-king's wife was dead, his old mother kept house for him and his six daughters. His youngest daughter was very quiet and thoughtful. And nothing pleased her more than hearing her grandmother tell stories about the far-off world of humans, about ships and towns and people.

"As soon as you are fifteen," her grandmother said, "you may rise to the surface of the sea and sit on the rocks and watch the ships sail by."

One by one the sisters turned fifteen, until at last it was the little mermaid's turn. Her grandmother put a wreath of white lilies and pearls on her head. The mermaid said good-bye, and she floated up through the water as lightly as a bubble.

When she came to the surface of the sea, the little mermaid saw the evening star shining in the pink sky. A three-masted ship was anchored in the water. There was singing and dancing on board; and as the night grew darker, hundreds of lanterns lit the deck.

The little mermaid swam about the ship, peeking in all the portholes. Every time she rose with the waves, she saw a crowd of people dancing. They were elegant and well-dressed. But the most striking of all was a young prince. He could not have been more than sixteen. How handsome he was—shaking hands with all the guests, laughing and smiling while beautiful music filled the night.

But as the little mermaid watched the prince, a sudden storm swept over the sea. The waves rose like mountains. The ship creaked and cracked. Water came rushing into the hold. Just as the ship broke in two, the prince fell into the deepest part of the sea.

The little mermaid swam through the dangerous waves until she reached the prince. She held his head above the water to keep him from drowning. At dawn, she carried him into a bay and laid him on the sand. Then she sang to him in her lovely voice. When she heard people coming, she hid behind some rocks.

A young girl appeared. She woke up the prince, and he smiled gratefully at her. He did not turn and smile at the little mermaid, though, for he had no idea that she was the one who had saved him and sung to him. Soon others came to help the prince, and he was carried away from the shore.

Thereafter, many evenings and many mornings, the little mermaid returned to the shore where she had left the prince. She saw the fruit ripen on the trees; she saw the snow melt on the high mountains—but she never saw the handsome prince.

At last she told the story to her sisters, and one of them showed her the palace where the prince lived. Thereafter, night after night, the little mermaid rose to the surface of the water and watched the gleaming palace. She even pulled herself up the marble steps, so she could gaze at the prince, standing on his balcony in the moonlight.

The more she visited the palace, the closer the little mermaid felt to humans, and she longed to be one of them.

"Do humans live forever?" she asked her grandmother.

"No," said the old lady. "Their lives are much shorter than ours.

We live for three hundred years, but when our lives come to an end, we turn to foam upon the water. But a human has a soul which lives on after the body dies. It flies up through the sky to the stars."

"Oh," breathed the little mermaid, "how can I get a human soul?"

"Well, if a human being loved you dearly and married you, you could get one," the grandmother said. "But that will never happen. The very thing that is so beautiful in the sea—your mermaid tail— is ugly and disgusting to humans."

The little mermaid looked sadly at her tail.

As time passed, the little mermaid could not forget her prince. One day she was filled with such longing that she made a terrible decision. "I will call on the sea witch," she said. She had always been afraid of the terrible witch, but now it didn't seem to matter.

The sea witch's house lay deep in the eerie sea forest. Her trees and bushes had long slimy arms that writhed like worms. Her yard was filled with fat water snakes slithering about. The witch's house itself had been built from the bones of shipwrecked humans.

"I know what you want," the sea witch said to the mermaid before she had a chance to speak. "You want to get rid of your fish's tail and have two walking stumps like humans have. You hope the prince will fall in love with you, and you'll be able to marry him and get a human soul." She let out a hideous laugh that sent her snakes sprawling to the floor of the sea.

"Well, I shall make a special potion for you," the witch went on. "Before the sun rises, you must carry it to the shore and drink it. Then your tail will divide into two parts. When those parts shrink into what humans call 'legs,' the pain will be almost more than you can bear. Though you will glide along more gracefully than any dancer, every step you take will be like treading on sharp knives. Are you willing to suffer this to be a human?"

"Yes," said the little mermaid.

"Remember, once you've taken a human shape, you can never be a mermaid again. Never be with your sisters or your father. If you fail to become the prince's wife, you won't be a human either! If he marries someone else, you will turn into foam the morning after his wedding. Are you willing to drink the potion and risk your life?"

"Yes," whispered the mermaid.

"And one more thing," said the witch. "You have the loveliest voice in the sea. I want it for my payment."

"But if you take my voice, what will I have?" the mermaid asked.

"Your beauty, your graceful movements, your speaking eyes. Now give me your voice, and I'll give you the potion."

"Oh dear, no," said the little mermaid. She was horrified at the thought of giving up her lovely voice.

"All right then," said the hideous sea witch, "you will *never* become human."

The little mermaid felt great despair. She didn't think she could bear to live if she didn't become human. "I will give up my voice if I must," she said sadly.

So the witch cut off the mermaid's tongue. Then she gave her a vial of magic potion. The drink glowed like a glittering star.

The little mermaid swam away from the horrible forest. When she saw her father's house, she felt as if her heart would break. She threw hundreds of kisses towards the palace. Then she rose up through the dark blue sea and swam to the prince's palace.

In the moonlight she made her way up the marble steps and drank the burning potion. A sword seemed to thrust itself through her body; and she fainted from the pain.

At dawn the little mermaid woke up. She felt the pain again. When she looked down at her fish's tail, she saw that it was gone. In its place were two beautiful white legs. She had no clothes on, so she wound her long hair around her body.

When the little mermaid looked up, she saw the prince standing before her. His coal-black eyes stared intensely at her.

"Who are you? Where have you come from?" he said.

The mermaid looked at him softly, yet sadly, for she could not speak. The prince took her hand, and led her to the palace.

The little mermaid was the fairest maid in all the kingdom and the prince was enchanted by her. They rode together on horseback and climbed mountains together. And when they went to parties, the little mermaid danced as no one had ever danced, and everyone marvelled at her graceful, flowing movements.

Sometimes, at night, the little mermaid crept down to the sea, and she heard the mournful song of her sisters as they swam over the water. In the distance, she saw her grandmother and her father stretching out their arms to her.

Though the prince was very fond of the little mermaid, he often seemed distracted, as if he were thinking of someone else. One night, he confided in her, "I'm in love with a girl I saw long ago. Once I was shipwrecked, and the waves carried me ashore. There a young girl found me and saved my life. She sang to me with her golden voice—a voice more beautiful than I've ever heard. I've never seen her since that day."

The mermaid felt great despair. Since she could not speak, she could not tell the prince what had really happened, that it was she who had saved him and sung to him.

Soon the mermaid heard a rumor that the prince was to be married to the daughter of a neighboring king.

"I am obliged to make a sea journey to meet this princess," the prince told the little mermaid. "My mother and father have insisted. But if I cannot find that girl who saved my life on the shore, I would like to marry you, my silent orphan with the speaking eyes." And he kissed her.

The prince and the mermaid journeyed together to the neighboring kingdom. In the moonlit night, the little mermaid sat by the ship's rail, gazing into the water. She thought she saw her father's palace and her grandmother's crown of pearls.

Soon the ship sailed into the harbor of the neighboring king's city. Church bells rang, and trumpets blared. The princess was brought to the ship.

When the prince looked upon her, he cried out with great joy. "It is you!" he said. "You're the one who saved me when I lay almost dead on the shore! My wish has come true!"

Indeed it was the girl who had discovered the prince on the shore. But the little mermaid would never be able to tell the prince that *she* herself was the one who had saved him from drowning at sea. She felt as if her heart would break.

The wedding ceremony was held immediately. The mermaid was dressed in silk and gold, and she held the bridal train. But she did not hear the festive music, nor pay attention to the ceremony. This was her last day in the world. The prince's wedding would soon bring her death; tomorrow she would turn to foam upon the sea.

That evening the bride and bridegroom slept in a royal tent on deck. The sails filled in the breeze; the vessel flew swiftly over the shining sea.

The little mermaid leaned her white arms on the rail and looked out to sea. Dawn would bring an end to her life. Suddenly she saw her sisters rising out of the water. They were as pale as ghosts, and their hair was cut off.

One sister held up a knife. "We gave our hair to the witch in return for help," she said. "She gave us this knife. When the sun rises, you must plunge it into the prince's heart. When his blood splashes on your feet, you will have a tail again. You can join us below in the sea. Hurry! Either he dies or you die."

The little mermaid took the knife and crept into the royal tent. She drew back the purple curtain and looked at the prince sleeping with his bride. She looked at the knife, then back at the prince.

The knife quivered in her hand. Suddenly she rushed out of the tent and hurled it into the sea. The waves shone red as though they were made of blood.

The little mermaid threw herself into the water. She saw lovely transparent creatures floating above her.

"You are one of us now," one of the lovely creatures said. "We are spirits of the air. We have no souls, but with good deeds we can win them. We fly to hot countries and send cool breezes to suffering people. We spread the fragrance of flowers. Then after we serve people for three hundred years, we are given a human soul."

The little mermaid felt great joy as she raised her arms towards the sun and floated through the water into the air. She saw the prince and his bride on the deck of the ship. They seemed to be searching for her.

Invisible to all, the little mermaid floated to the ship. She kissed the bride and smiled at the prince. Then she rose like a pink cloud high into the morning sky.

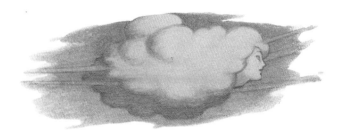

AUTHOR'S NOTE

OST of these stories can be classified as folktales. Folktales are stories which are handed down orally from one generation to another; they served primarily as entertainment and were told on long winter nights before the fire, in the nursery, at the spinning wheel, in taverns, and on pilgrimages. The story of the Sea Nymph and the Cyclops is a myth as it is derived from the story of Galatea, a character in ancient Greek mythology. The stories of Melusine and Menana might be classified as actual legends for they were originally told as explanations of certain historical phenomena. Lastly, the Little Mermaid and the Princess of the Tung Lake are literary inventions, for they were derived primarily from the writing of a single author.

I've included the following notes which further explain the source of each story:

The Mystery of Melusine is a French legend that dates back to the fourteenth century. According to Gwen Benwell and Arthur Waugh, authors of *Sea Enchantress,* Melusine was the most popular of all medieval legends. "She was regarded as anything but a legendary figure in the Middle Ages, and the noble families in France down to the humble peasantry believed in her implicitly." My source for this retelling was *Curious Myths of the Middle Ages,* by Sabine Baring-Gould, published in 1868.

Menana of the Waterfall was inspired by the legend "The Island of Eagles" in *Traditions of the North American Indians,* by James Athearn Jones, published in 1830. After much searching, I was thrilled to finally find this three volume collection in the reserve library at the Museum of Natural History in New

York. Jones traveled among Native American tribes, transcribing their stories and traditions. Though he does not clearly specify what tribe relayed the story of Menana to him, he indicates that it came from the Ottawas of the Canadian forests.

The Sea Nymph and the Cyclops was adapted from the story of Galatea and Polyphemus in *Metamorphoses,* completed in 8 A.D. by the Latin poet, Ovid. Ovid's tale retells a Greek myth first told by the Alexandrian poet Theocritus around 250 B.C. Ancient Greek mythology has many nymphs of rivers, streams, and oceans, including the fifty Nereids who lived in the Aegean Sea. Galatea is one of the best known of the Nereids.

The Enchanted Cap is a retelling of the folktale, "The Lady of Gollerus," a story collected by Thomas Croker in the early 1800's and anthologized in *Fairy and Folk Tales of Ireland,* edited by W.B. Yeats in 1892. In his notes, Yeats explains that the Irish believed that the sea fairy — or *Merrow* — was not an uncommon sight on their wilder coasts. The *Merrow* wore a red cap called a *cohuleen druith.* If it was stolen, she would be unable to return to her world under the waves.

Nastasia of the Sea was derived from the folktale "The Story of Tremsin, the Bird Zhar, and Nastasia, the Lovely Maid of the Sea," from *Cossack Fairy Tales and Folk Tales,* edited by R. Nisbet Bain in 1894.

The Fish Husband. I am indebted to Sharon Dennis Wyeth for finding "The Beautiful Girl and the Fish," in *Fourteen Hundred Cowries,* a collection of Yoruba folktales retold by Abayomi Fuja. Born in Nigeria in 1900, Abayomi Fuja's parents were Yorubas from Offa. He says, "It is a custom among all Yoruba people to gather children together, especially on moonlit nights, and relate these stories to them...."

The Serpent and the Sea Queen was adapted from "Toda, the Archer, and the Queen of the World Under the Sea" from a collection of folktales titled *Wonder World,* by Marie Pabke and Margery Deane, 1877. Their footnote to the story quaintly reads: "This story, which is a very ancient and famous one, has been put into its present English dress by Prof. William E. Griffis, the author of *The Mikado's Empire* — the latest and the most complete work on Japan."

The Mermaid's Revenge was adapted from the folktale, "The Mermaid's Vengeance" in *Popular Romances of the West of England, or the Drolls, Traditions, and Superstitions of Old Cornwall,* collected and edited by Robert Hunt in 1908. Of this story, Hunt says: "Several versions of the following story have been given me. The general idea of the tale belongs to the north coast [of Cornwall]; but the fact of mermaidens taking innocents under their charge was common around the Lizard, and in some of the coves near the Land's End."

The Princess of the Tung Lake was derived from "The Princess of the Tung-T'ing Lake" written by the seventeenth-century Chinese scholar P'u Sung-ling and collected in *Strange Stories from a Chinese Studio,* translated by Herbert A. Giles and published in Shanghai in 1916.

The Sea Princess of Persia was adapted from the folktale "Julnar the Sea-born and her Son" in *The Thousand Nights and One Night* (also known as *The Arabian Nights*), translated by Sir Richard Burton in 1885–1886. The collection of tales in *The Arabian Nights* can be traced to three distinct cultures: Indian, Persian, and Arab. Some of the tales are over a thousand years old.

The Mermaid in the Millpond was adapted from "The Nixie of the Millpond" from Grimms' Fairy Tales. The German nixie — or *wasser-nixen* — is a water sprite who lives in rivers or lakes and sometimes has a fish tail. Germanic folklore has many other water maidens, including swan-maidens and the Lorelei, a water spirit of unearthly beauty who haunted the Rhine.

The Little Mermaid is a retelling of "The Little Mermaid" written by Hans Christian Andersen in 1837. Though Andersen gathered and retold old folktales, *The Little Mermaid* was an original story. In the last one hundred and fifty years, it has been adapted for opera, ballet, and motion picture, as well as immortalized in paintings, sculptures, and statues all over the world.

ARTIST'S NOTE

HEN I first visualized the art for this book, naturally I pictured it in the romantic realistic style that characterizes my work. But as time went on, I discovered my approach was changing. The deeper I delved into the stories, the more convinced I became of the need to illustrate each one in a style representative of its place of origin. Finally, I couldn't visualize it any other way.

Soon, the stacks of reference books grew higher and higher around my studio. I made trips to the library and trips to museums to make reference sketches of works of art. In the process, I became more familiar with the unique art and culture of each country or civilization I would be depicting.

Working in the various modes was an adventure for me. As my paintings transported me from one culture to the next, I entered the world and psyche of artists from each time and place.

In the Japanese tale, I became a gentle, steady-handed Japanese artist as I applied fragile sheets of gold leaf and then impressed them with the tip of a stick.

With the "The Sea Nymph and the Cyclops," I became as a fourth-century Grecian, painting on terra-cotta with a restricted palette. I painted figures that were totally flat, silhouetted shapes set against a solid color, a landscape represented only by two curved lines. In contrast, for the nineteenth-century Danish tale, "The Little Mermaid," I gave the art depth and a modeling effect by creating a light source that illuminated the clouds and cast indirect shadows. Colors were reflected in the water; each element had its own texture.

I noticed how sixteenth-century Persian miniatures had a cut-and-paste kind of look. The perspectives were pressed flat, and pieces of what looked like wallpaper seemed to have been placed randomly in the composition. Yet, as I imitated the style, I realized how carefully planned the figures, colors, and geometric shapes were.

While the styles of the sixteenth-century Persian art and fifteenth-century French illuminated manuscript art look quite different, they also had, I discovered, some of the same characteristics: a flattened or distorted perspective, decorative qualities, scenes that show cutaway views of rooms, lettering, and touches of gold leaf incorporated into the art.

My research for the African piece was a tactile experience. In African art, from ancient times to the present, decorative designs appear on pottery, clothing, and buildings—and were usually found on something functional that had been carved, then painted over. I took elements of the designs I found, then applied them two-dimensionally for my illustration. The diamond design that I used on the initial cap at the opening of the tale was one that I saw often.

In the art history of many countries, a variety of styles exist. In those cases, I chose genres that I felt were best suited to the particular narrative. In "The Enchanted Cap," for example, I depicted the Mermaid of Gollerus in the folk art tradition one might find on a pub sign. The Ukrainian tale is in the style of Bilibin, an Eastern European book illustrator who worked during the turn of the century. The art for the Native American story shows the character Menana as though seen through the eyes of an artist-explorer. In addition to all the other skills and tasks an explorer had to perform, these pioneers recorded a civilization that was soon to disappear. Along with their articles of survival, they carried sticks of charcoal for drawing or small boxes of watercolors. The initial cap and character endpiece for the story represent the bark cut-outs that the Native People of the North Eastern woodland made as patterns for beadwork designs.

Signing each painting proved to be intriguing for me as well. Often, signatures in book illustrations can be distracting and unnecessary. But many of the styles I was portraying had signatures as a noticeable element. The seals or stamps that appear in Japanese and Chinese art are good examples of this technique. Some of the fifteenth- and sixteenth-century German artists, Albrecht Dürer in particular, worked their names, initials, and dates into pictures on stone or signs hanging from twigs; other times they just had them float in the sky. Some of the early American explorers recorded information about their subjects on the art itself, along with their signatures and dates, with the flourish of a quill pen. Where the signature was not part of the genre, I imagined the type of personality the artist might have had and signed the work accordingly, as in the Irish and English pieces.

Working on this book has provided me with a unique opportunity to understand the art and artists of other times and places. I hope these pictures spark some interest and help readers appreciate our rich global artistic heritage.

T · Howell

BIBLIOGRAPHY

Andersen, Hans Christian, *Andersen's Fairy Tales*, New York: Grosset & Dunlap, 1945.

Anson, Peter F., *Fisher Folk-lore*, London: The Faith Press, 1965.

Bain, R. Nisbet, *Cossack Fairy Tales and Folk Tales*, London: Lawrence and Bullen Publishers, 1894.

Baring-Gould, Sabine, *Curious Myths of the Middle Ages*, London: Rivingtons, 1868.

Bassett, F.S., *Legends and Superstitions of Sailors and the Sea*, Chicago & New York: Belford, Clarke & Co., 1885.

Beck, Horace, *Folklore and the Sea*, Middletown: Wesleyan University Press, 1973.

Benwell, Gwen, & Waugh, Arthur, *Sea Enchantress*, New York: The Citadel Press, 1965.

Burton, Sir Richard (translator), *The Thousand Nights and One Night*, New York: Heritage Press, 1934.

Fuja, Abayomi, *Fourteen Hundred Cowries*, London: Oxford University Press, 1962.

Giles, Herbert, A., (translator), *Strange Stories from a Chinese Studio*, Shanghai: Kelly & Walsh, 1916.

Grimm, Jakob, *Grimms' Fairy Tales*, London: Routledge and Kegan Paul Ltd, 1948.

Humphries, Rolfe, (translator), *Metamorphoses*, by Ovid, Bloomington: Indiana University Press, 1955.

Hunt, Robert, *Popular Romances of the West of England*, London: Chatto & Windus, 1908.

Jones, James Athearn, *Traditions of the North American Indians*, London: Colburn and Bentley, 1830.

Jung, Emma, *Animus and Anima*, New York: Analytical Psychology Club, 1957.

Ozaki, Yei Theodora, *Japanese Fairy Book*, Archibald Constable & Co. Ltd, 1903.

Pabke, Marie & Deane, Margery, *Wonder World*, New York: E.P. Putnam's Sons, 1877.

Rhys, Sir John, *Celtic Folklore*, Oxford: Clarendon Press, 1901.

Yeats, W.B., *Fairy and Folk Tales of Ireland*, London: Smythe, 1973.